Fact Finders®

PEOPLE YOU
SHOULD KNOW

RUBY BRIDGES

Get to Know the Girl Who Took a Stand for Education

by M. Michelle Derosier

CAPSTONE PRESS
a capstone imprint

Fact Finders are published by Capstone Press,
1710 Roe Crest Drive, North Mankato, Minnesota 56003
www.mycapstone.com

Library of Congress Cataloging-in-Publication Data
Library of Congress Cataloging-in-Publication data is available on the Library of Congress website.

ISBN 978-1-5435-5527-1 (library binding)
ISBN 978-1-5435-5925-5 (paperback)
ISBN 978-1-5435-5537-0 (ebook PDF)

Editorial Credits:
Mari Bolte, editor; Kayla Rossow, designer; Svetlana Zhurkin, media researcher;
Tori Abraham, production specialist

Photo Credits:
AP Images, 16, 22; Getty Images: Bettmann, cover, 5, 20, 25, 27, Paris Match/Paul Slade, 12, The Boston Globe/Lane Turner, 19, The LIFE Images Collection/Carl Iwasaki, 8, The LIFE Images Collection/Don Cravens, 14, Underwood Archives, 15, 18; Library of Congress, 7, 26; Newscom: Everett Collection, 11, Sipa USA/Van Tine Dennis, 28; Official White House Photo by Pete Souza, 29
Design Elements by Shutterstock

Source Notes
p. 4, line 14: Jonann Brady. "First New Orleans Black Student: Hardships Worth It." https://abcnews.go.com/GMA/Inauguration/story?id=6680876&page=1. Accessed on July 5, 2018.

p. 6, line 5: Ruby Bridges. *Through My Eyes.* New York: Scholastic Press, 1999, page 6

p. 17, line 9: Michelle Miller. "Ruby Bridges, Rockwell Muse, Goes Back to School." https://www.cbsnews.com/news/ruby-bridges-rockwell-muse-goes-back-to-school/. Accessed on July 13, 2018.

p. 18, image caption: Kimberly Harms. "Remembering Former U.S. Marshal Charles Burks, Who Protected 6-year-old Ruby Bridges." http://www.prweb.com/releases/2017/07/prweb14474156.htm. Accessed August 9, 2018.

p. 18, line 9: Eileen McClusky. "Ruby Bridges Evokes Tears, Smiles as She Tells Her Tale. https://news.harvard.edu/gazette/story/2002/04/ruby-bridges-evokes-tears-smiles-as-she-tells-her-tale/. Accessed August 3, 2018.

p. 23, line 7: Katy Reckdahl. "Fifty Years Later, Students Recall Integrating New Orleans Public Schools." https://www.nola.com/politics/index.ssf/2010/11/fifty_years_later_students_rec.html. Accessed August 8, 2018.

p. 24, line 1: Whitney Hales. "Ruby Bridges Speaks on Civil Rights at BYU." https://universe.byu.edu/2015/11/20/ruby-bridges-speaks-on-civil-rights-at-byu1/. Accessed May 4, 2018.

p. 25, line 9: *Through My Eyes*, page 50.

p. 26, line 11: Ibid., page 50.

p. 26, line 21: Ibid., page 53.

p. 27, line 10: Ibid., page 57.

p. 28, line 8: Kasey Jackson. "Ruby Bridges: A Purposeful Life." http://www2.kiwanis.org/docs/default-source/kiwanis-magazine/archive-issues/ki-0117.pdf. Accessed August 9, 2018.

p. 29, line 14: William Allman. "President Obama Meets Civil Rights Icon Ruby Bridges." https://obamawhitehouse.archives.gov/blog/2011/07/15/president-obama-meets-civil-rights-icon-ruby-bridges. Accessed August 7, 2018.

Printed in the United States of America.
PA48

TABLE OF CONTENTS

1 ▶ THE FIRST DAY

There were no happy faces to welcome six-year-old Ruby Bridges to her first day at William Frantz Elementary School. But there were **federal** marshals—and a crowd.

"Two, four, six, eight, we don't want to integrate," the crowd chanted. Some of them threw things at Ruby and her mother, Lucille. Others tried to block the entrance to the school. Ruby made it through the doors, but it wasn't much better when she got inside. No students talked to Ruby. No teachers welcomed her to class. And parents pulled their children out of school throughout the day. "Over five hundred kids left school that day," Ruby said later.

Groups gathered to protest at William Frantz Elementary throughout the school year.

Until November 14, 1960, William Frantz had been an all-white school. Ruby was the first African American student to attend. She didn't understand it at the time, but she would become the symbol to the United States that all children, regardless of their race, deserve equal education.

federal—having to do with the national government in Washington, D.C.

Ruby Nell Bridges was born on September 8, 1954, in Tylertown, Mississippi. Her parents and grandparents were **sharecroppers** on a farm. Lucille knew she wanted her children to do something else. "Sharecropping is hard work," she said. "On the day before Ruby was born, I carried 90 pounds of cotton on my back. I wanted a better life for Ruby."

When Ruby was four years old, her parents moved to New Orleans, Louisiana. Her father, Abon, worked as a service station attendant. Her mother cared for the children during the day. At night, she took different jobs, including housekeeping at a hotel.

The family did not have a lot of money. They rented two bedrooms of a house. Other families lived in other parts of the house. Ruby and her siblings shared a single room piled with bunk beds.

The first school for previously enslaved people was built in 1863. The first black high school opened in 1870.

Despite being crowded, Ruby's life was carefree. She had fun jumping rope, climbing trees, and playing softball. Ruby attended kindergarten at Johnson Lockett Elementary, a **segregated** school with black teachers and students. Her teacher, Mrs. King, reminded Ruby of her grandmother in Mississippi.

Little did Ruby know that while she was living her childhood, adults were making decisions that would affect her future.

sharecropper—a person who works farm fields for an owner in exchange for a small part of the profits

segregated—separated by race

BROWN V. BOARD OF EDUCATION

In 1951 a black man named Oliver Brown sued the local board of education in Topeka, Kansas. He wanted his daughter Linda to attend an all-white school.

Linda Brown (left), her parents, Leona and Oliver, and her little sister, Terry, in 1953

Brown's lawyers presented an argument that segregation put black children at a disadvantage. Schools were supposed to be separate but equal, but they were not. The board said black and white students did get the same level of education.

The year Ruby was born, the United States **Supreme Court** ruled on *Brown v. Board of Education*. They said that segregating schools was wrong.

When?

The Supreme Court did not specify how integration was supposed to happen, or when. In 1955 the Court passed a second ruling, called *Brown v. Board of Education II*. All nine Supreme Court justices agreed that states needed to start **desegregating** their schools as soon as possible. But they again did not give a deadline. The responsibility for **integration** was on lower courts and school districts. This let some states to put off integration for a long time. In 2015—60 years after *Brown*—more than 180 school districts were involved in active desegregation cases.

Supreme Court—the most powerful court in the United States

desegregate—to get rid of any laws or practices that separate people of different races

integrate—to bring people of different races together in schools and other public places

The most vocal and violent opposition to the *Brown v. Board of Education* ruling came from **segregationists**. They believed that the U.S. Constitution couldn't force them to integrate. If people were segregated, it was by choice. In their opinion, it would take black students time to catch up to their white peers once schools were integrated. These ideas were rooted in racism. The segregationists did what they could to preserve the ways of life they were used to.

Segregationists delayed integrating schools as long as they could by ignoring the ruling. Those at local levels of government took funding away from schools that tried to integrate, forcing them to close. White families moved away to mostly white neighborhoods or paid to start private schools that allowed only white children. Those who supported desegregation had their businesses or lives threatened.

The Little Rock Nine

On September 4, 1957, nine black students integrated Central High School in Little Rock, Arkansas. The opposition was fierce and violent. More than 1,000 white people gathered outside in protest, shouting threats and throwing stones. National Guard soldiers, sent by the governor, blocked the door. The Little Rock Nine weren't able to enter the school.

They tried again on September 25. The Nine were able to get into the building through a side door, but had to leave soon after when the crowd outside became too violent. President Dwight D. Eisenhower sent 1,200 U.S. Army troops from the 101st Airborne Division to protect the Nine for the rest of the school year.

The Little Rock Nine had their lives threatened daily. The army was there to protect them on the way to and from class, but soldiers were not allowed in bathrooms, locker rooms, or classrooms.

segregationist—a person who believes people of different races should be kept apart

The segregationists used every tool available to deny black children an equal education. The New Orleans school board created a standardized test. They said it would determine which black students were smart enough to attend white schools. However, the test was purposely very difficult. The board hoped it would be too difficult to pass.

Five-year-old Ruby and about a hundred other students took the test together. Ruby was one of the few to pass. She and five other kindergarteners were chosen to start first grade at a white school.

Ruby, with her parents, Abon and Lucille, in their kitchen, 1960

Ruby's parents had a difficult decision to make. Should they risk putting their daughter in danger for a chance at a better education and future? Abon, who had fought in the Korean War (1950–1953), had little faith in integration. He and other black servicemen risked their lives alongside white soldiers. But they had separate sleeping quarters and ate in separate halls. After serving their country, they came back to a segregated United States. If soldiers willing to fight and die alongside each other couldn't integrate, he did not see a future where it would ever happen. And he did not want to put his family in jeopardy.

Lucille, however, believed differently. Members of the National Association for the Advancement of Colored People (NAACP) encouraged her to see integration as access to more opportunities for the future. She believed that attending William Frantz would open doors not only for Ruby, but for generations of African American children to come. In the end, Lucille and Abon agreed that Ruby would go to the all-white school in September 1960.

segregationists carried a Confederate flag during a protest at the Louisiana State Supreme Court Building in 1960

Segregationists in Louisiana believed the government did not have the right to tell them how to live. At all levels of their state and local government, they took action to block integration. Anyone who argued with segregationists could be fined or jailed. Schools where mobs formed or **riots** broke out could be closed. Governor Jimmie H. Davis threatened to close all public schools rather than see them integrated. These tactics kept Ruby and the other children from starting at their new schools. One of the children changed their mind. Now there were four.

But the federal court, led by Federal District Court Judge J. Skelly Wright, was even more determined to uphold *Brown v. Board of Education*. It was time for every state in the United States to recognize and respect black Americans as equal citizens. The judge set a new date of Monday, November 14, for school integration in New Orleans.

DID YOU KNOW?

The first black children who would integrate white schools were first graders. Leona Tate, Tessie Prevost, and Gail Etienne would attend McDonogh 19. Ruby would be the only black student at William Frantz.

Gail Etienne was escorted to McDonogh 19 by Federal Marshal Wallace Downs.

riot—a large gathering of people who use violence to show their anger

A LONG WALK

The long-awaited first day of school had arrived—November 14, 1960.

That morning, four federal marshals came to escort Ruby and her mother to the school. Although the school was just five blocks away, Ruby would need protection. Lucille told Ruby that there might be a lot of people outside. But Ruby didn't really know what to expect.

Policemen were there to protect Ruby and anyone else inside the school. Later, they set up barriers around Ruby's street to protect the Bridges' home.

Barricades and human bodies surrounded the building. At first, Ruby thought they were there for a Mardi Gras parade. But the angry faces were not there to celebrate.

Some **protesters** carried signs. Others shouted **slurs** at Ruby and her mother, and spat at them as they walked by. One person carried a small coffin with a black baby doll inside. "I used to have nightmares about the coffin," Ruby recalled. Many of the protesters were young, working-class mothers whose children attended the school. They called themselves "cheerleaders."

With the marshals' help, Ruby made it into the building. She spent the first day in the principal's office as angry parents pulled their children out of school.

barricade—a wall or other type of barrier used to keep people out

protester—someone who objects to something strongly and publicly

slur—insulting name or word

On the second day of school, Ruby was allowed to go to class. Most of the teachers refused to teach while Ruby was in the school. But one was more than willing.

"I had never seen a white teacher before, but Mrs. Henry was the nicest teacher I ever had," Ruby said later. While the protesters shouted outside, Mrs. Henry began to teach her class of two. Ruby sat at the front of the room and Lucille was in the back.

After the first two days, Lucille stayed at home. Ruby went to and from school alone with the marshals.

The Last Teacher

Barbara Henry was from Boston. She had taught at desegregated schools for years before coming to William Frantz. She believed that her whole life had, in a way, prepared her for teaching Ruby.

Mrs. Henry had taught in military schools overseas. Those schools were all integrated. After she married an Air Force lieutenant, they moved to New Orleans. Two months later, she was hired at Ruby's school.

As Ruby's teacher, Mrs. Henry wanted to protect her from the ugly world outside. She worked hard to make the classroom as normal as possible, and to make Ruby feel welcomed and wanted. She said the year was "long, solitary, and wonderful. Our only classmates were the federal marshals at the door."

In 2014 Barbara Henry shared her story with a newspaper. She holds a photo of herself and Ruby from 1960.

Violent clashes between both sides increased and protesters were sent to the hospital. People threw bricks or flaming bottles of gasoline at passing cars. The Ku Klux Klan (KKK) burned crosses in black neighborhoods. Parents were warned to keep their children in at night.

an angry woman protesting integration at William Frantz Elementary in December 1960

But people showed compassion toward the Bridges family during this time too. The Bridges received cards and letters with kind, supportive messages. Some sent money and gifts. Even former first lady Eleanor Roosevelt wrote them a personal note.

Ruby's neighbors stopped by often. They took turns standing guard outside the Bridges' house at night to make sure no one tried to break in. The neighbors helped Ruby get ready in the morning or walked with the marshals to school. They pitched in to babysit during the school break. One even hired Ruby's father as a housepainter.

DID YOU KNOW?

Nearly 300 white children in the St. Bernard Parish school district did not receive a formal education in 1960. Despite other opportunities outside of William Frantz and McDonogh 19, some parents chose to keep their children home all year.

As the weeks went on, white parents continued to keep their kids away from school. Some parents sent their children to a neighboring school instead. A rich segregationist donated money and a building to form a new white-only private school.

However, a few white parents felt differently. Reverend Lloyd Foreman believed that integration was spiritually and **morally** right. He insisted that his daughter, Pam, attend her regular school.

Police escort the Foremans through an angry crowd in late November 1960.

Another white student, Yolanda Gabrielle, stayed too. But even though Pam, Yolanda, and Ruby were the only students at the school, they were each taught in different classrooms. This continued when other students returned too. Yolanda said she only saw Ruby once. "That's the irony of this: We were still kept segregated," she said.

Tough Times

Supporting integration had a price. Lloyd Foreman received bomb threats. His church and home were **vandalized**. For many years, people challenged his decision. Yolanda's mother was shouted at and called names. School board president Lloyd Rittiner lost so much work he nearly went bankrupt. He was threatened and his property damaged. Ruby's grandparents lost the land they sharecropped. Her father lost his job. The family was even banned from shopping at their local grocery store.

moral—an ability to choose between right and wrong

vandalize—to damage property

5 ▸ ALL ALONE

"The worst part about first grade for me was the loneliness," Ruby said later. She couldn't go outside for recess. When she had to go to the bathroom, a marshal came with her. On her second day of school, one woman threatened to poison her. Because of that, she was only allowed to eat food from home. But she soon stopped eating at school altogether, wanting to join the other students in the cafeteria.

Child psychiatrist Dr. Robert Coles volunteered to meet with Ruby and the three black students who attended McDonogh 19. He came to Ruby's house every week. He had her draw pictures of herself, the school, and the people in her life. They used the pictures to talk about her feelings.

Listening to Ruby led Dr. Coles to seek out and listen to other children around the country.

Toward the end of the year, Ruby finally met some of the white children who had returned to the school. But what should have been a happy time wasn't. One of the boys refused to play with her. He called her a slur, saying, "My mama said not to because you're a n----r." Before that day Ruby didn't really understand **racism** or integration. But in that moment she understood what all the protests, the anger, and the separation were about. "I finally realized that everything had happened because I was black," she said.

racism—treating people differently because of a belief that some races are better than others

Ruby

When June finally rolled around, the school year ended quietly. Ruby received excellent grades. However, the principal claimed that was because Mrs. Henry gave her so much individual attention. The principal's comment didn't matter. To Ruby, nothing she said could take away from "what was in my head."

When Ruby returned to school for second grade, much had changed. The marshals were gone. So were the protesters. Sadly, so was Mrs. Henry. Ruby did not learn until years later that her favorite teacher had moved back to Boston to raise her family. Ruby's class that year included some black students. But Ruby found it hard to adjust. "From second grade on, I felt different from the other kids in my class," said Ruby.

Ruby graduated from an integrated high school but did not go to college. It was a decision she would always regret, although she would later receive honorary degrees. She took a job as a travel agent. Ruby was one of the first African Americans to work for American Express in New Orleans.

She married and had four sons. Her sons attended integrated schools in a New Orleans, a city she described as "less racist than it used to be."

Ruby in 1982

The Ruby Bridges Foundation's goal is to teach tolerance, appreciation of differences, and respect. Today Ruby (left) travels to schools around the country to spread her message of equality.

In 1999 Ruby established The Ruby Bridges Foundation. The foundation works toward safe schools and quality education for everyone. Her memoir, *Through My Eyes*, was published that same year.

Ruby is determined to help the United States become less racist. She travels across the country speaking to kids. "If we're going to get past our racial differences, it's not going to come from us. It's going to come from our kids."

The Story Goes On

Ruby's life and story have been captured in art, books, and on screen. A statue of her was built in the schoolyard of William Frantz in 2014.

The most famous representation is the Norman Rockwell painting "The Problem We All Live With." In it, six-year-old Ruby is marching with her book in hand, her back straight, and her head held high. She is surrounded by her team of marshals. The terrible word that racist protestors constantly shouted at her is scratched onto the wall.

In 2010, on the 50th anniversary of that life-changing walk, Ruby was invited to the White House. The nation's first African American president, Barack Obama, had the painting there. "If it wasn't for you guys, I wouldn't be here today," he told Ruby.

President Barack Obama and Ruby viewing "The Problem We All Live With" in July 2011

GLOSSARY

barricade (BA-ruh-kade)—a wall or other type of barrier used to keep people out

desegregate (dee-seg-ruh-GAYT)—to get rid of any laws or practices that separate people of different races

federal (FED-ur-uhl)—having to do with the national government in Washington, D.C.

integrate (IN-tuh-grate)—to bring people of different races together in schools and other public places

Mardi Gras (MAR-dee GRAH)—last day of Carnival, a two-week celebration that includes parades, parties, and feasts

moral (MOR-uhl)—an ability to choose between right and wrong

protester (pro-TEST-uhr)—someone who objects to something strongly and publicly

racism (RAY-siz-uhm)—treating people differently because of a belief that some races are better than others

riot (RYE-uht)—a large gathering of people who use violence to show their anger

segregated (SEG-ruh-gay-ted)—separated by race

segregationist (seg-ruh-GAY-shuhn-ihst)—a person who believes people of different races should be kept apart

sharecropper (SHAIR-krop-ur)—a person who works farm fields for an owner in exchange for a small part of the profits

slur (SLUR)—insulting name or word

Supreme Court (suh-PREEM KORT)—the most powerful court in the United States

vandalize (VAN-duhl-ize)—to damage property

READ MORE

Bridges, Ruby. *Through My Eyes*. New York: Scholastic Press, 1999.

Hood, Susan. *Shaking Things Up: 14 Young Women Who Changed the World*. New York: HarperCollins, 2018.

Llanas, Sheila. *Children in the Civil Rights Era*. Mendota Heights, Minn.: Focus Readers, 2018.

INTERNET SITES

Use FactHound to find Internet sites related to this book.

Visit *www.facthound.com*

Just type in 9781543555271 and go.

 Super-cool stuff!

Check out projects, games and lots more at
www.capstonekids.com

CRITICAL THINKING QUESTIONS

1. At first, Ruby did not understand the impact her actions had. Later, though, she realized that she was part of something big. Re-read the text. When do you think this realization happened?

2. Ruby believes in the importance of teaching and knowing an event's true history. Think about *Brown v. Board of Education*. Do you think both sides of the story are presented in the text? Explain why or why not.

3. Think back to when Ruby was a child. Have things changed since then? Explain why or why not.

INDEX